Learning to Think Critically:
The Case of Close Relationships

A Handbook to accompany

PSYCHOLOGY

Third Edition

Carole Wade and Carol Tavris

▟ HarperCollins*CollegePublishers*

Learning to Think Critically: The Case of Close Relationships, A Handbook to accompany Wade/Tavris PSYCHOLOGY 3e

ISBN: 0-06-500522-8

92 93 94 95 96 9 8 7 6 5 4 3 2

Do you think critically? Chances are you do. Every day, each of us must evaluate information in order to make judgments and reach decisions. This process is at the heart of critical thinking. Unfortunately, however, we do not always evaluate information correctly, nor do we always draw conclusions that are well-supported. In this handbook, we will show you some critical thinking strategies that can make you a better thinker and a better consumer of psychological findings. We will do this by applying critical thinking to a sphere of life that all of us care about very much, the sphere of close relationships. However, these strategies are applicable to virtually *any* problem in human life, be it practical, personal, or political.

WHAT IS CRITICAL AND CREATIVE THINKING?

How many times, in the midst of a rousing quarrel with friends, parents, or strangers, have you encountered the following styles of argument--all of which illustrate failures of critical thinking?

- "Just shut up about this, OK? You don't know what you're talking about."

- "I don't care what your so-called evidence is. Anybody can find any survey to support anything they want it to."

- "Don't argue with me. I'm older than you are and I know from personal experience that I'm right."

- "My feelings are very strong on this point, so don't try to change them."

- "I was raised to believe that . . ."

In critical thinking, a person identifies *reasons* to support or reject an argument or belief. Feelings aren't enough, personal experience or anecdotes aren't enough, and shouting down the opposition isn't enough. Critical thinkers are willing to question received wisdom and ask why things are as they are. They are willing to think creatively about alternative ways of doing things or explaining them. They understand that it is important to define terms, examine the evidence, and analyze assumptions and biases. They try to avoid emotional reasoning (as in "That argument makes me feel uncomfortable, so it must be wrong") and oversimplification (as in "All the evil in the world is due to that small group of loathsome people"). And they tolerate uncertainty; no one can ever know all the answers to every problem, and even when we think we have some answers, we must be prepared for them to change when new

2

information or new circumstances appear. (On page 3 you will find a reference list of these guidelines for thinking critically and creatively.)

In this handbook, we will demonstrate how psychologists have used critical thinking strategies in their studies of close relationships and suggest ways that you can apply these strategies to your own experiences. The subject of love and intimacy has produced many "common sense" notions and barrels of folklore, but are common assumptions true? Do opposites attract? Is passionate love the key to a happy marriage? Do breakups occur primarily because of "incompatibility"? Are men more likely than women to be bullies and women more likely than men to be manipulative in getting their way?

We will show how psychologists have gathered information about such questions, and have tested and evaluated possible answers -- in short, how they have applied critical thinking to what, for most people, is an emotional topic. In addition to practicing your critical thinking skills, you may find some surprising answers to your questions about what attracts people to each other, keeps them together, and causes them to break up.

GUIDELINES FOR THINKING CRITICALLY AND CREATIVELY

1.<u>Ask questions; be willing to wonder</u>. To think critically you must be willing to think creatively -- to be curious about the puzzles of human behavior, to wonder why people act the way they do, and to question received explanations and examine new ones.

2.<u>Define the problem</u>. Identify the issues involved in clear and concrete terms, rather than vague ones such as "happiness," "potential," or "meaningfulness." What does meaningfulness mean, exactly?

3. <u>Examine the evidence</u>. Consider the nature of the evidence supporting various approaches to the problem under examination. Is it reliable? Valid? Is the "evidence" merely someone's personal assertion or speculation? If the evidence is scientific in nature, does it come from one or two narrow studies, or from repeated research?

4.<u>Analyze biases and assumptions</u> -- your own and those of others. What prejudices, deeply held values, and other personal biases do you bring to your evaluation of a problem? Are you willing to consider evidence that contradicts your beliefs? Be sure you can identify the biases of others, as well, so you can evaluate their arguments.

5.<u>Avoid emotional reasoning</u> ("If I feel this way, it must be true"). Remember that everyone holds convictions and ideas about how the world should operate, and that your opponents are probably as serious about their convictions as you are about yours. Feelings are important, but they should not substitute for careful appraisal of arguments and evidence.

6.<u>Don't oversimplify</u>. Look beyond the obvious. Reject simplistic, Be alert for logical contradictions in arguments and be wary of "argument by anecdote."

7.<u>Consider other interpretations</u>. Before you leap to a conclusion, think about other explanations. Be especially careful about drawing conclusions about cause and effect.

8. <u>Tolerate uncertainty</u>. Possibly the hardest step in becoming a critical thinker, for it requires the ability to accept some guiding ideas and beliefs -- yet the willingness to give them up when evidence and experience contradict them.

Critical thinking begins with a willingness to ask creative questions about human experience. For example, we all meet thousands of people during a lifetime. Have you ever wondered why some become central characters in our lives while others remain bit players, or stay offstage altogether?

Assumption: *We are attracted to people for their special qualities. We seek out those who are witty, wise, kind, or attractive, and our excellent judgment recognizes their good qualities.*

Thinking critically: Your text (Chapter 18) points out that most people concentrate on personal qualities and dispositions when trying to explain their own or someone else's behavior, and ignore the effects of the situation and the environment. Critical thinking demands that we overcome this bias, and consider external as well as internal influences on attraction. Certainly not everyone is compatible with everyone else. But there are over five billion people on this earth, and for any one person, there are many others who would qualify as an appealing partner. What must happen before two individuals actually get together?

In the process of gathering evidence on this question, psychologists have established that people are often drawn to each other for the most mundane of reasons: simple proximity. That is, they happen to be in the same place at the same time. They may live in the same neighborhood, attend the same classes, take the same bus every morning, or work for the same company. Spatial proximity makes people available and reduces the costs of pursuit, in terms of time and effort. If the person lives too far away, becoming better acquainted may not be worth the effort-- which is why people in some parts of the country talk about a potential date as being "G.U.," geographically undesirable.

Proximity also makes people familiar, and, according to research, familiarity tends to breeds comfort rather than contempt. In a classic study of proximity, researchers plotted the development of friendships in a new housing project for married students (Festinger, Schachter, & Back, 1950). The students, who were initially strangers, lived in two-story buildings with five apartments to a floor. The closer the students lived to one another, the better friends they became. Other research has shown that geographical distance per se is less important than frequency and ease of contact. People who live near stairways, courtyards, and entrances, where people are always going in and out, have more friends than people who live in the same building but outside the flow of traffic (Monge & Kirste, 1980; Newcomb, 1961). In a classic series of experiments on the effects of "mere exposure," Robert Zajonc (1968) showed that even very brief repeated encounters with other people (or, for that matter, objects and even nonsense syllables) increase our feelings of attraction toward them.

Think critically about these findings, however; do not just passively absorb the information, or overgeneralize to all situations. If proximity can increase the opportunity for friendship and romance, it can also increase the opportunity for conflict and hostility. Not only our lovers but also our enemies are likely to be people with whom we are in close proximity (Ebbesen, Kjos, & Konecni, 1976).

To apply critical thinking you should also look for the implications of research. One implication of the proximity principle is that if you live in an isolated room, house, or apartment, and you want to meet more people, you should consider ways to get yourself in the flow of traffic. If you can't move your living quarters, you might move yourself to more populated environments. It makes no sense to be angry that the world isn't beating a path to your door; this is human nature. How often do you go out of your way to visit distant friends?

Before going on, can you think of any other implications of the research on proximity?

Assumption: *Opposites attract.*

Thinking critically: Critical thinking includes looking for logical contradictions. Is the notion that opposites attract consistent with the principle we have just discussed, the proximity principle? Think about it: people find themselves in physical proximity because they do the same work, have chosen the same sort of neighborhood to live in, or share some common hobbies or ambitions. Thus people who bump into each other all the time are likely to have interests, activities, and backgrounds in common. This fact is inconsistent with the notion that opposites attract.

Psychologists have called the "opposites attract" idea the *complementarity principle*. (To complement means to balance or make whole.) The complementarity principle predicts that people will seek friends or spouses who have some quality that they lack or that balances the qualities they have (Winch, 1958). However, much of the evidence on this notion is negative. In one famous study of 321 dating couples in Boston (henceforth referred to as the "Boston Couples study"), those who eventually broke up were less well-matched in age, educational ambitions, intelligence, and physical attractiveness than those who stayed together (Rubin, Peplau, & Hill, 1981). Another study, of 108 married couples, tested the common belief that traditionally masculine husbands (aggressive, individualistic, ambitious, decisive, and dominant) are happiest with traditionally feminine wives (cheerful, sympathetic, warm, tender, and nurturant toward children), and that such wives are happiest with traditionally masculine husbands (Antill, 1983). The researcher found no support for the "opposites attract" idea. Instead, the happiest couples were those in which

7

both spouses scored high on "feminine" traits, qualities that are especially useful in marriage and child rearing.

An alternative to the complementarity principle is the *matching principle*, which predicts that people will seek out and be attracted to those who are similar to them in looks, interests, intelligence, education, age, family background, religion, attitudes, and values (Burgess & Wallin, 1943; Byrne, 1971; Murstein, 1982). This principle has been supported by scores of studies. Birds of a feather really do flock together, whether they are mating, dating, or just out for a lark.

Why should like attract like? One reason is that similar people belong to the same *field of eligibles*, or pool of potential intimates, in terms of the socially "correct" religion, class, education, and age (Winch, 1958). The field of eligibles for an individual is defined by social norms and may change over time. For example, interracial and interreligious marriages, and marriages between older women and younger men, are no longer as taboo as they once were.

If you are thinking critically, however, you might ask yourself whether, despite these findings, there might be some qualities for which complementarity does apply. The critical-thinking approach rejects simplistic either-or thinking and calls for a continual refining of hypotheses. It is reasonable to suppose, for example, that in such funda-mental areas as class, education, values, and sexual desire, similarity matters a great deal, whereas in daily living, complementarity in certain personality traits may be useful. Two extremely ambitious people may find it more complicated and stressful to live together than a couple in which one person is professionally ambitious and the other is not. Or it may help when one likes to cook and another to eat, or when one likes to garden and the other to vacuum.

Moreover, complementarity may be more important to some people than others. In one study, researchers found that for couples who were generally hostile rather than friendly, marital satisfaction and security were highest when one partner was relatively dominant and another relatively submissive (Campbell & Brown, 1990). The researchers speculate that for hostile people, complementarity may be a way of avoiding conflict. Perhaps that is why, in couples therapy, conflict between partners often increases when a formerly submissive partner begins to be more assertive.

In science, questions are never closed, and new discoveries often depend on admitting some uncertainty. Further research may find that similarity and complementarity both operate in successful relationships, but in different ways, and at different stages of the relationship.

Assumption: *"You can't judge a book by its cover" because "beauty is only skin deep."*

Thinking critically: Folk sayings, which are supposed to reflect the common wisdom, may hide as well as reflect the truth about human behavior. "Money isn't everything" and "The best things in life are free" are two bits of popular wisdom, yet all too often, people are so busy trying to accumulate wealth that they have no time for all of those free "best things." Could the denial of beauty's importance in folk sayings similarly mask an anxious concern about it? Why do we idolize glamorous celebrities and portray villains as ugly?

As psychologists have gathered evidence on these questions from naturalistic and laboratory studies, they have discovered that physical appearance influences the reactions of others literally from the moment an infant emerges from the womb ("Look at that gorgeous head of hair!" "Oh dear, he's as homely as a plucked chicken"). Parents, teachers, and playmates tend to give more attention and praise to children who are good-looking than to plainer children, and this bias continues into adulthood (Berscheid, 1985). It may be unfair and undemocratic, but

9

physical attractiveness is one of the strongest determinants of attraction. It is so strong, in fact, that when the "book" has an unattractive cover, many people may not bother turning to the first page of a relationship.

It is hard for many people to acknowledge the importance of beauty in their choices of friends and lovers. But if we think critically, we will be cautious about using self-reports of attitudes as a valid guide to how people really feel. When college students are asked to rank the attributes that are important to them in a potential date, they almost never put looks at the top of the list. But what they say is not always consistent with what they do. In a classic study, Elaine Hatfield and her associates randomly matched 752 college students for a "computer dance." The researchers had assessed each student's intelligence, aptitudes, social skills, personality traits, and physical attractiveness. During an intermission at the dance, and again a few months later, the students were asked in private how much they liked their dates. The only variable that predicted their answers was attractiveness. The researchers, thinking that looks would be only one aspect of a date's desirability, diligently examined every possible factor. But they could not argue with the data: No matter how they analyzed the results, looks mattered most (Walster et al., 1966).

Men, according to several studies, are more likely than women to say they prefer good-looking partners, yet when people are asked to rate their actual attraction to other people, *both* sexes tend to give the partner's looks a high priority (Feingold, 1990; Sprecher, 1989). One reason is the physical attractiveness stereotype. People who hold this stereotype do not really believe that beauty is only skin deep; they think it reflects the whole person. When they are asked to judge attractive or unattractive individuals whom they have never met, they tend to assume that the attractive ones are more sensitive, more interesting, more popular, more dominant, more poised, more outgoing, more sexually responsive, happier, mentally healthier, more intelligent, and on and on (Berscheid, 1985; Feingold, 1992).

10

Sometimes stereotypes have a kernel of truth. Could it be that when we expect good-looking people to have nice qualities, we treat them especially nicely, thereby fostering the development of all those nice qualities and bringing about a self-fulfilling prophecy? This hypothesis has been a popular one among social psychologists, and it makes sense -- but "making sense" is not enough. Critical thinkers want evidence before they will draw conclusions. The first step, then, is to find out whether good-looking people really do have all those terrific traits that others tend to credit them with. In recent research, Alan Feingold (1992) used a statistical technique called meta-analysis to assess the results of numerous studies on this question. He found that good-looking people do tend to be somewhat more popular, more socially skilled, and less lonely and socially anxious than other people. However, the physical attractiveness stereotype greatly exaggerates the positive qualities of physically attractive people: for most of the mental abilities and personality traits that have been studied, the correlations are trivial or nonexistent. As Feingold puts it, "Good-looking people are not what we think."

These findings on physical attractiveness may seem discouraging for the majority of us who are ordinary-looking. But critical thinking requires us to examine all sides of an issue. When we do so, we see, first, that the beautiful have problems too. The physical attractiveness stereotype is not completely positive: Very attractive people are sometimes assumed to be vain, egocentric, less intelligent, or snobbish (Dermer & Thiel, 1975). Second, the beautiful are sometimes assumed to be unavailable or aloof when they are not. Third, our subjective ratings of our own physical attractiveness often don't match the judgments of others -- and it is our self-perceptions that are critical for social and romantic success. When people think of themselves as good-looking (whether others agree or not), they tend to have high self-esteem and good mental health, to be outgoing and comfortable in social situations, and to be popular (Feingold, 1992).

Most important, almost everyone, whether good-looking or not, does find friends and a mate. Based on what you have read so far, can you find

11

reasons why this should be so? Remember the matching principle. It predicts that in the real world, people will tend to select friends and lovers whose attractiveness roughly matches their own. And indeed, that is what people do; they minimize the chances of rejection by choosing partners who are like themselves in attractiveness (Feingold, 1988). However, it is also possible that good-looking people get "first pick," selecting one another as mates and leaving less attractive people to choose from the remaining field of eligibles (Kalick & Hamilton, 1986).

You can apply critical thinking in your own life by being wary of the physical attractiveness stereotype, which may be limiting your choice of friends or blinding you to people's real qualities. If you are thinking critically, you are questioning assumptions -- in this case, the very definition of beauty.

This country is made up of many racial and ethnic groups--African-Americans, Swedish-Americans, Native Americans, Asian-Americans, and Latinos, just for starters--and how many of them end up in psychological studies? Members of different races and cultures have differing ideas about what physical attributes qualify as "beautiful": which skin color, hair texture, shape of eyes, degree of plumpness (and where it is located). The cultural practices that define a "beautiful look" are enormously varied, from piercing the earlobe to piercing the nose, from dreadlocks to ponytails.

For this reason we must ask: Just who is defining what is beautiful, anyhow? In every culture, the group having the most power is the one that defines general standards of attractiveness, and those standards become widely shared. Therefore, it can be difficult for minorities to accept their own attributes if these are not considered "beautiful" by the majority. Critical thinking requires us to consider that our feelings about beauty may originate in social norms and outside circumstances, and may not be due simply to individual feelings or preferences.

Assumption: *True love means being selfless, and always placing your partner's needs above your own.*

Thinking critically: Does this idealistic notion jibe with the laws of human behavior? If you refer to Chapter 6 of your text you will find that reinforcements, or rewards, are powerful controllers of behavior. Rewarded behavior is likely to continue; unrewarded behavior is likely to disappear, or be "extinguished." In light of this fact, is it reasonable to assume that people "truly in love" can continue in a relationship with no thought of reward? The evidence reveals that, in fact, good relationships depend on a two-way, or reciprocal, exchange of rewards and punishments (Homans, 1961; Thibaut & Kelley, 1959). People do not enter or stay in relationships without any thought of what they will be getting from them.

Other people have the power to bestow all sorts of rewards: praise, affection, sexual pleasure, entertainment, help, good company, and insurance against loneliness. They can also bestow punishments: They can be demanding, irritable, intrusive, and impose financial burdens. According to *social exchange theory*, when two people embark on a relationship or consider whether to stay in one, they mentally compute what they can get from each other and what they have to offer in return.

Sometimes, of course, people begin or stay in relationships that others see as unrewarding. These cases do not necessarily contradict social exchange theory, however. If you stop to define your terms, in this case the meaning of a reward, you will find that "reward" is a relative term. A drop of water is extremely rewarding if you have been lost in the desert for three days, but not so rewarding if you've been camped by a spring. A job transfer that increases your pay but reduces your free time is rewarding if you are low on funds, but not so rewarding if you are rich. Similarly, an offer of friendship will mean more to someone who is lonely than to someone whose social calendar is always full. What one person perceives as rewarding is not necessarily rewarding to another.

13

The exchange that people compute when deciding whether to begin or stay in a relationship, then, is not selfless; in some ways, it is like an economic transaction. The "bottom line" of the balance sheet is affected by your *comparison level*, the standard against which you evaluate the costs and rewards of the relationship (Thibaut & Kelley, 1959). That standard, in turn, depends on what you expect from a relationship and what you think you deserve. If the other person gives you more than you expect or feel you deserve, you will be attracted to that person (if you're starting out) or satisfied with what you have (if you're already in a relationship). If the other person gives you less than you expect or feel you deserve, you will not pursue the relationship or you will feel dissatisfied with an existing one.

Attraction to others -- and willingness to remain in a relationship once it has begun -- also depends on your *comparison level for alternatives*. This is the lowest standard you will accept in light of what you believe is possible in other relationships. People often remain in relationships that they know are unsatisfactory, continuing to live with people they find unpleasant and difficult, because they believe they have no better alternative. Teresa may be surly and critical, yet Tom may stay with her if he thinks he cannot do better and doesn't want to be alone. (For some other reasons that people stay in relationships that appear to be unrewarding, see the Epilogue of your text.)

Popular songs and stories often equate "true love" with selflessness, self-sacrifice, and even suffering. But if you are thinking critically, you will distinguish the cultural ideal from what really is so. It is true that many people are capable of great selflessness in their close relationships. However, the evidence shows that it is normal to want to receive as well as give in a love relationship. This is why the *principle of reciprocity*, which holds that we tend to like those who like us, may be the strongest principle of all in explaining attraction (Berscheid & Walster, 1978). By looking for signs that another person thinks well of you, you minimize the chances of being hurt by rejection, and you enhance your self-esteem.

14

Can you think of a way to apply the principle of reciprocity? One application might benefit lonely people, who tend to focus their attention on themselves and their unhappiness. When they meet a new person, they are so worried about the impression they are making that they become self-absorbed. They may assume in advance that the new person won't like them, even when this isn't true. To avoid the pain of rejection, they may develop a pattern of "rejecting others first" (Jones, 1982). This is not the best way to make a new friend! It simply creates another self-fulfilling prophecy. How might the lonely person break out of this cycle? One way is to give to others what he or she hopes to get: attention, interest, and support.

As you were reading about the principles and rules of attraction, perhaps you found yourself quarreling with some of the conclusions in this section. You may know a Beauty who married an adoring Beast. You may know a commuting couple who defy the laws of proximity, maintaining a relationship across many miles. You may know an extrovert who has been happily married for 42 years to an introvert. If you are questioning the generalizations in the preceding section, that's good; it means you are actively evaluating what you are reading, which is what this booklet is all about.

However, apparent exceptions to the rules of attraction do not necessarily invalidate them. For one thing, when people make choices about which relationships to pursue, they don't necessarily count every factor equally (Berscheid, 1985). The importance of any one influence depends on an individual's needs. A person may decide that looks are nice, but less important than a kind nature, or power, or money. A commuting couple may put up with the inconvenience of distance, because his ability to play the tuba and hers to play the flute allows them to make beautiful music together.

Second, the general determinants of attraction interact with individual personality traits. One such trait is *self-monitoring*, the self-conscious need to observe and control one's image in social situations (Snyder, 1987). In one study, young men were given the choice of going out with one of two dates. "Kristen" was described as plain-looking but friendly and outgoing. "Jennifer" was described as good-looking but self-centered and moody. Most men high in self-monitoring chose Jennifer, despite her grumpy personality. But most men low in self-monitoring men chose Kristen (Snyder, Berscheid, & Glick, 1985). Apparently men who are concerned about their own social image are also concerned with a date's. Men who do not shift their images to suit the occasion are more interested in a date's inner qualities.

Remember, then, as you apply general principles of attraction in your own life, that critical thinkers avoid oversimplification. The influence of any principle depends both on the situation and on an individual's needs and beliefs.

> ## GROWING CLOSER:
> ## THE DYNAMICS OF INTIMACY

As two people grow closer, certain changes occur in their relationship. Chief among them are the establishment of equity, an increase in self-disclosure, and a strengthening of commitment.

Assumption: *In a close relationship, all benefits and obligations should be shared equally.*

Thinking critically: In everyday life, "fairness" or "equity" is often confused with a strict 50-50 division of benefits and obligations (paying half the rent, doing half the chores, giving equal gifts, and so forth). If you analyze the concept of equity carefully, however, you will see that it is not that simple. As we have noted, social exchange theory predicts that people will try to maximize the rewards they receive in a relationship. But they will judge those rewards in light of what they, themselves, can offer a partner. Thus fairness does not always mean that two partners must receive exactly equal benefits.

According to equity theory, in order to see a relationship as fair, two partners must believe that each person's benefits are proportional to what he or she contributes to the relationship (Walster, Walster, & Berscheid, 1978). Equity results when the ratio of costs to benefits is perceived to be the same for both people--when the more a person puts in, the more he or she gets out. Suppose we can measure costs and benefits on a scale of one to ten. Norma's contribution to a relationship may be worth only a two and her rewards only a four, while Nat's contributions may earn a five and his benefits a ten. But since the ratio for each of them is the same ($2/4 = 5/10$), both will feel that the relationship is equitable.

Research finds that people in equitable relationships are generally happier and more content than those in inequitable ones (Hatfield et al., 1985; Sprecher, 1986). Partners who are "underbenefited," who feel they are getting less than they deserve, are apt to feel angry or depressed. (For most people, it seems, too much selflessness quickly leads to feelings of resentful martyrdom.) Some studies have found that people don't like being "overbenefited" either, and that when they think they are getting more than they deserve, they may feel guilty or depressed (McElfresh, 1982; Schafer & Keith, 1980). Women seem especially likely to feel uncomfortable with being overbenefited. Other studies, however, find that overbenefited partners are as happy and satisfied with their relationships as equitable partners are (Traupmann et al., 1981). When there is a conflict like this in the data, critical thinking requires us to wait for more evidence before drawing any conclusions.

17

Again, you may be able to think of some apparently happy relationships that are not equitable. Does that invalidate equity theory? Before you decide that the theory is no good, consider some alternative explanations. First, in long-term relationships, the goal is not usually immediate repayment for everything one does, but fairness over the long haul. A spouse, for instance, may be willing to live with an inequitable balance during a specific phase of life (say, when rearing young children or starting a new career), in the confidence that equity will eventually be restored (Traupmann & Hatfield, 1983). Second, it is the perception of equity that matters, rather than the objective state of affairs; in the absence of actual equity, people may be able to convince themselves that equity exists (Brehm, 1992). Partner A may decide that partner B deserves the greater benefits, because he or she is "special" and A is merely ordinary. Or partner A may have a comparison level for alternatives that makes A feel well treated compared to others of the same gender, even if B doesn't really deserve all those extra benefits. Moreover, in long-term relationships, fulfilling the other person's needs may be experienced as rewarding, even when doing so entails considerable "costs" (Clark & Reis, 1988).

There is, however, another problem with equity theory. The finding that "the most happily married couples have the most equitable relationships" is correlational, and critical thinking prevents us from drawing conclusions about causation from findings that are correlational (see Chapter 2 of your text). Equity may cause happiness, but it is also possible that happiness causes equity -- or the perception of equity. That is, happy couples may be especially likely to emphasize the fair aspects of their relationships. Once a couple becomes dissatisfied, they may begin to attend to issues of unfairness that were previously swept under the rug. At present, then, we cannot be sure that equity causes happiness, or that inequity brings discontent, although we suspect that both are true.

Assumption: *Women are the "intimacy experts"; men are afraid of intimacy.*

Thinking critically: In order to evaluate an assumption critically, we must examine the way we define our terms. The truth of this particular assumption depends on what we mean by intimacy.

If we equate intimacy with verbal disclosure of personal feelings, thoughts, and weaknesses, then there is some truth to this common assumption. When men talk to each other or to women, they tend to talk about relatively impersonal matters, such as cars, sports, work, and politics. When they reveal anything about themselves, it tends to be their strengths and achievements. Women are more likely to talk about personal matters, such as their feelings and relationships, and are more willing to reveal weaknesses, fears, and worries (Hacker, 1981; Tannen, 1990).

There are other ways to define intimacy, however. It turns out that both men and women want intimacy, but they often have different ideas about self-disclosure as a way of achieving it. Many men in our culture define "intimacy" with a partner as shared activities and having sexual relations (Cancian, 1987). In contrast, women are more likely to define intimacy as shared revelations of feeling. As noted in Chapter 9 of your text, men tend to want "side-by-side" relationships (doing things together) and women tend to prefer "face-to-face" relationships (revealing ideas and emotions). This sex difference begins early. A study of 300 eighth-graders found that boys expressed intimacy with other boys through shared experiences, typically group activities such as football. The girls, however, preferred one-to-one conversations. The researchers found that shared experiences were just as effective as self-disclosure in engendering feelings of closeness (Camarena & Sarigiani, 1985).

These differences in male and female styles of intimacy reflect traditional gender roles in American culture. Men are as able as women to have "intimate" conversations when the situation makes it desirable for them to

19

do so (Reis, Senchak, & Solomon, 1985). Both sexes are equally likely to report wanting intimate friends, and the same men who fear self-disclosure with their male friends are often happy to disclose to their romantic partners. But on average, gender roles encourage different styles of intimacy in men and women, and these differences are often a source of tension between them. "Why doesn't he talk more?" the woman laments. "Why doesn't she shut up?" the man wonders. In one study, husbands were instructed to increase the frequency of expressions of love toward their wives, and the wives were asked to keep track of such demonstrations. One husband, asked by the researcher why he hadn't complied with the instructions, replied huffily that he certainly *had* complied--by *washing his wife's car*. The husband thought that was a perfectly good way to communicate love for his wife, but she hadn't a clue to his intentions (Wills, Weiss, & Patterson, 1974).

To think critically we must examine and evaluate our own values and judgments. Critical thinking leads us to recognize that the same behavior can be regarded as good or bad, depending on your point of view. In her book *Intimate Relationships*, Sharon Brehm (1992) observes that a man who is emotionally inexpressive may be regarded as calm and steady or as cold and unresponsive. A woman who is emotionally expressive may be regarded as warm and responsive or as hysterical and flighty. When people talk about sex differences in intimacy, their biases often get in the way. Each sex, of course, thinks that its way of doing things is the better way.

If we can overcome our biases and the temptation to reason emotionally, we may find that there are positive and negative aspects to each gender's preferred form of intimacy (Tavris, 1992). As we note in Chapter 15 of your text, social support is an important element in mental and physical health, and women have more sources of social support than men do. In part, this is because women are more likely than men to seek and to give emotional comfort (both to men and to other women). Both sexes feel better after talking things over with a woman (Burda, Vaux, & Schill,

20

1984; Wheeler, Reis, & Nezlek, 1983). Disclosing one's feelings often helps the discloser feel understood, validated, and cared for (Reis & Shaver, 1988).

However, the female emphasis on self-disclosure also has disadvantages. The constant ventilation of an emotion often rehearses the feeling instead of getting rid of it (see Chapter 9). Could this fact be related to the finding that emotional disorders, such as anxiety and depression, are more common among women than among men? Perhaps when women endlessly discuss their fears and worries, they make themselves more fearful and anxious. Men, by suppressing their fears and forcing themselves to act, may conquer their anxiety. Perhaps, too, dwelling on the problems in their relationships sometimes allows women to avoid taking action to improve them (Nolen-Hoeksema, 1991).

"Intimacy" is one of those nice warm words that sounds good, but critical thinking requires us to avoid oversimplification. As Elaine Hatfield (1984) has observed, there are certain dangers in too much self-revelation and certain pleasures in privacy. When people reveal their weaknesses and wants, they risk being abandoned, having their revelations betrayed to others, provoking anger or contempt in their partners, and losing their individuality. If men sacrifice intimacy (in the sense of self-revelation) because they fear loss of independence, women may sacrifice independence because they fear loss of intimacy.

You can see that critical thinking leads us far from the simpleminded notion that one sex has the edge on intimacy.

Assumption: *All you need is love.*

Thinking critically: The truth of this assumption, like the truth of the previous one, depends on how you define your terms. For many people in our culture, love is largely synonymous with romantic passion. The

21

secret of a lasting relationship is thought to be keeping passion alive. Yet in almost every culture, proverbs recognize and lament the inevitable death of passion. "A dish of married love grows soon cold," say the Scots. "Love makes the time pass. Time makes love pass," say the French. "Love and eggs are best when they are fresh," say the Russians.

In this case, research confirms what proverbs observe: No intense emotion lasts forever. Tempers cool, elation ebbs, hurt evaporates, and romantic passion fades (Berscheid, 1985; Botwin, 1985; Solomon, 1988). As two people become familiar with each other, their relationship loses the element of novelty and surprise. As a result, the physiological arousal they once felt in each other's presence declines. This is probably necessary for survival. A constant state of romantic excitement would produce enormous wear and tear on the body, to say nothing of making it difficult to read, work, or wash the dishes.

Consider the practical implications of this finding. In many cultures, marriage is viewed as a contractual arrangement between two families; love has nothing to do with it. But in our culture, marriage has been largely divorced (so to speak) from its economic purposes, and people are free to marry for love. Most couples expect romance not only to precede the wedding but to continue for a lifetime afterwards. Yet passion is bound to subside. As we note in Chapter 10 of your textbook, when that happens, a couple may be disappointed and disillusioned. "The divorce rate is so high," says Robert Sternberg (1985), "not because people make foolish choices, but because they are drawn together for reasons that matter less as time goes on."

Clearly, if you want your relationship to survive, love -- in the sense of romantic passion -- is not enough. The forces that bring a couple together have little to do with the forces that keep them together. Grand passion, it seems, is like fireworks on the Fourth of July: spectacular but fleeting. Sternberg (1988) notes that love in the fullest sense includes not only passion, but intimacy and commitment. Passion is an emotional element,

22

involving high arousal and energy. Intimacy involves the motivation to be close to the loved one. Commitment is a cognitive element, consisting of the judgment that one is in love, the decision to become committed, and attitudes about the other person. The amount of love we feel, in Sternberg's view, depends on the strength of these three components. The kind of love we feel depends on the strengths of each relative to the others. Thus you might have a commitment to a lover -- an intention to maintain the relationship -- but feel little passion. Or you might have intense emotions toward a lover, but not be mentally prepared for commitment.

For lovers and spouses in our culture, commitment usually means an agreement not to "shop around" for another relationship. Recent research suggests that people in committed relationships resist temptation by actually altering their own perceptions of other potential partners. They tend to minimize the positive personality traits of other potential partners, especially very attractive ones (Johnson & Rusbult, 1989). Heterosexual people in committed relationships are also less likely than uncommitted individuals to judge members of the other sex as physically and sexually attractive (Simpson, Gangestad, & Lerma, 1990). And they pay less attention to, and show less interest in, potential alternatives; as researchers Rowland Miller and Jeffry Simpson (1990) note, "even if the grass is greener elsewhere, happy gardeners may not notice." (The converse, however, could also be true: If you don't think too much about attractive alternatives, you may have a better chance of being happy in your own garden!)

Committed partners save the time, money, and effort they would otherwise spend on "shopping," and in turn gain emotional security and confidence that the relationship will continue. (Are you reading actively? Can you relate this observation to social exchange theory?) A commitment may be expressed publicly, which is what weddings are for, or it may be a private decision.

23

Considering the importance of commitment, it is surprising how little research has been done on it. However, over the past decade, psychologists have started to investigate this important element of successful relationships. In one study, 351 happy couples who had been married for at least 15 years were asked what had kept their unions alive and well. Husbands and wives put the belief that marriage is a long-term commitment near the top of the list. These couples expressed a determination to work through their problems, and to endure some temporary unhappiness while they were doing it. As one man, married for 20 years, said, "I wouldn't go on for years and years being wretched in my marriage. But you can't avoid troubled times. You're not going to be happy with each other all the time. That's when commitment is really important" (Lauer & Lauer, 1986).

We still do not know all the factors that allow some people to make a commitment and others not. However, commitment seems to be tied more closely to trust than to romantic love. In interviews with dozens of couples happily married for many years, Francine Klagsbrun (1985) found that trust came up over and over again. "Feelings of love may wax and wane in the course of a marriage," she observed, ". . . but trust is a constant; without it there is no true marriage." Each partner must trust that the other will be there, will protect confidences, and will offer support and safety. In a sample of 47 couples (married, cohabiting, or dating, with an average age of 30), researchers found that the most important aspect of trust was faith, the belief that one's partner will act in loving and caring ways, whatever happens in the future (Rempel, Holmes, & Zanna, 1985).

These findings on love and trust should cause you to think about the implications in your own life. Are many grand passions worth the stability of one trustworthy one? Do people in our culture overvalue romance? Perhaps there is another kind of love, one that is more intense than mere affection but more permanent than a brief, whirlwind passion. Perhaps people in successful long-term relationships experience what we might call "romantic sentiment," an ability to seek and enjoy novelty in each other, and to maintain a sense of courtship and surprise.

TROUBLED WATERS: THE DYNAMICS OF CONFLICT

What do you think makes a relationship "close"? Psychologists have come up with several answers to this question. But according to many theorists, when you boil them all down, what's left at the bottom of the definitional pot is *interdependence* (Kelley et al., 1983). Interdependence refers to the ability of two people to influence each other's plans, thoughts, actions, and emotions. The degree of closeness depends on how often the participants influence each other, how many areas of their lives are affected, and how intensely they are affected.

Yes, you say, but what about all those warm fuzzy feelings we've just discussed, feelings of intimacy, trust, respect, and love? To be sure, close relationships usually do involve positive emotions -- but not all the time. In ongoing relationships, people have the power to affect each other in negative as well as positive ways, sometimes simultaneously. The more time two people spend together, the more they have to disagree about, and the more opportunities there are for disappointment, hurt feelings, and conflict. As Elaine Hatfield (1984) has noted, "The opposite of love is not hate, but indifference."

The way a couple resolves their differences affects the quality of their relationship and its chances of survival. Let's examine some common assumptions about how people deal with differences, and about what happens when their efforts fail.

Assumption: *As Carl Jung once said, "Where love rules, there is no will to power; and where power predominates, there love is lacking."*

Thinking critically: This assumption is a charming one, but unfortunately it isn't true. Like the assumption that true love is selfless, it describes an ideal rather than an actual state. Power is the ability to influence decisions and get other people to do what you want. By that definition, lovers are as likely as anyone else to use and abuse their power. In the Boston Couples study, 95 percent of the women and 87 percent of the men thought that both partners should have exactly equal say, yet fewer than half thought that their own relationships were equal. When one person had more say, it was the man in 40 percent of the cases and the woman in only 15 percent (Peplau, 1984).

Why do you think men tend to have more power in a relationship? A first guess might be that men understand power better, or that men are trained to exercise power whereas women are trained to be more submissive or cooperative. But remember, critical thinking requires that we consider other less obvious explanations, such as factors external to personality, when explaining behavior. One such factor is a person's resources. In general, the greater a person's resources, the greater his or her power. A resource is anything that can be used to satisfy or frustrate the needs of others, or move them toward or away from their goals (Huston, 1983). Resources include education, income, skills, occupational prestige, sexual desirability, and physical strength. The more resources an individual has in the family, the greater his or her power. In most of these areas, particularly income and education, husbands have traditionally had the edge, and therefore more power to make decisions. When a couple's resources are more balanced, so is the distribution of power.

When wives are employed and contributing directly to the family's standard of living, their resources and power rise. For decades, this finding has turned up consistently in studies of families (Blood & Wolfe,

26

1960; Blumstein & Schwartz, 1983; Hochschild, 1989). But why do full-time homemakers, who contribute to the family by caring for children, organizing the housework, and providing emotional support, have so much less power than spouses who bring in money? To understand this issue, we must go beyond simplistic notions, such as "men are male chauvinists" or "women want to be dominated." Such explanation don't tell us much. A more illuminating analysis may be that in the United States, people's value is often measured by their economic worth (Waring, 1988). Most people do not recognize the financial value of work performed in the home. (How many families could afford to hire a full-time cook, babysitter, decorator, housekeeper, dishwasher, and chauffeur?) Another possibility is that the goal of equity actually diminishes a homemaker's power. As we said earlier, what people feel entitled to in a relationship depends on what they are contributing. In many families, economic contributions count heavily in the equity equation. The result is a sadly modern version of the Golden Rule: Those that have the gold make the rules.

Consider the implications of these arguments. If power is related to resources, and particularly financial ones, then there is nothing inherently female about lack of power or inherently male about having it. That hypothesis is borne out by evidence. When men are "househusbands," staying home to raise the children while their wives earn the family income, the wives have greater power (Beer, 1984). Among gay and lesbian couples, there is no expectation based on gender that one partner will be "the boss," yet power in gay relationships is often lopsided. As in heterosexual relationships, it is the partner who has more resources, and in particular a higher income, who tends to have more power (Blumstein & Schwartz, 1983).

Money, however, isn't the only determinant of power. According to the *principle of least interest*, the person with the least need to continue a relationship has the greatest influence and control in it (Waller, 1938). The degree of interest depends in part on how attracted the two partners

27

are to each other and how emotionally dependent they are. He may be a millionaire oil magnate and she a struggling secretary, but if he is wildly in love with her and she is merely mildly interested in him, she will have greater power (though his millions may last longer than his feelings).

If you are actively considering the implications of these findings, you may be wondering how power is related to satisfaction. A few studies find that satisfaction is high when the husband has more power and greater say in decisions. This seems to be especially true in studies of young black couples, perhaps because the wives are sensitive to the occupational and economic barriers that black men face in our society and wish to cushion and protect their husbands' self-esteem and sense of masculinity (Acitelli, Douvan, & Veroff, 1990). The choices we make in our close relationships do not occur apart from the social context we live in.

Most studies, however, find that a high degree of marital satisfaction and stability are associated with roughly equal power in decision making (Gray-Little & Burks, 1983). When either spouse has most of the power, arguments and even violence are more frequent than in families in which both spouses feel they have influence (Yllo, 1983). Both sexes are particularly uncomfortable and dissatisfied when the woman has the greater power. Why might this be so? One factor is the cultural expectation that men should be dominant. Another is that many of the wives who assume authority do so by default rather than by mutual agreement. That is, they pick up the reins of power when their husbands are physically ill, unemployed, or unwilling to be involved in family life.

It would be nice to believe that "love can conquer all," but critical thinking requires us to question cherished ideas when the evidence contradicts them. In this case, the evidence suggests that emotional involvement cannot be separated from financial realities.

Assumption: *To get their way, men shout or give orders and women cry or give hints.*

Thinking critically: There is some truth to this assumption. Men are more likely than women to give orders directly ("Lock the door"), women to give them indirectly ("Would you mind locking the door?") (Lakoff, 1990; Tannen, 1990). And in dating and marriage, the sexes do tend to use different strategies for getting their way. Influence strategies may be *direct* (saying what you want) or *indirect* (dropping hints). They may also be *bilateral* (requiring interaction with your partner) or *unilateral* (requiring only your own action). Psychologists have found that men are more likely than women to use strategies that are direct and bilateral, such as reasoning and bargaining. Women are more likely than men to use strategies that are indirect and unilateral, such as pouting, crying, or withdrawing (Falbo & Peplau, 1980). Men are also more likely to use what some researchers call "hard" strategies (demanding, shouting, being assertive), whereas women are more likely to use "soft" strategies (acting nice, flattering the other person) (Kipnis & Schmidt, 1985).

These findings jibe with stereotypes about men and women. Both sexes expect women to cry, sulk, be "nice," be "emotional," and use flattery or manipulation if necessary. Both sexes expect men to show anger, call for logic and reason, be "rational," and use force if necessary. But, as we have shown in previous sections, an apparent sex difference may be due to something other than gender itself. To think critically, we must always look beyond the obvious to find the forces that actually account for some phenomenon. Failure to do this is a common weakness in people's thinking.

Given our preceding discussion, you might already have some idea of what lies behind sex differences in strategies of influence. Research has found that these differences are related less to gender than to power (Carli, 1990; Lakoff, 1990). Lesbians and gay men do not differ from each other in the techniques they favor (Falbo & Peplau, 1980). Bilateral

29

strategies are used by people who have the greater power and status in a relationship, whatever their gender or sexual preference. Powerless people prefer indirect strategies in order to avoid angering their partners by direct confrontation -- or simply in order to please them.

For example, Linda Carli (1990) observed pairs of individuals -- male-male, male-female, and female-female --discussing a topic on which they disagreed. Women spoke more tentatively than men did, she found, only when they were speaking to men! With men, they offered more disclaimers ("I'm no expert," "I may be wrong," "I suppose," "I mean," "I'm not sure"). They used more hedges and moderating terms, like the use of *like* ("Drinking and driving is, like, dangerous"). And they used more tag questions that solicit agreement ("It's unfair to prevent 18-year-olds from drinking when they can be drafted and killed in war, isn't it?").

Carli even discovered why many women use such hesitations and tags when they speak with men: It works. Women who spoke tentatively were more influential with men and less influential with women," she reports. Tag questions and hesitations annoyed other women, but they seemed to reassure the men. Even though the men regarded an assertive woman as being more knowledgeable and competent than a woman who says the same thing but with hesitations, they were more *influenced* by a woman who spoke tentatively. They liked her more and found her more trustworthy. When a woman uses tentative language with a man, Carli concludes, she may be communicating that she has no wish to enhance her own status or challenge his. This makes him more inclined to listen.

People who share decisions and power tend to bargain rationally and to make compromises. These couples tend to be the most satisfied with their relationships. Unlike users of hard tactics, they do not alienate their partners and create hostility or fear. Unlike users of soft tactics, they do not lose self-respect (Kipnis & Schmidt, 1985).

Assumption: *Most couples break up because of incompatibility. They just "didn't get along."*

Thinking critically: This assumption is an example of what logicians call a *tautology*, a statement that is true by definition but doesn't really say anything. All the assumption says is that when couples don't get along it's because . . . they don't get along. It tells us nothing about *why* people fail to get along.

Research finds that happy couples and distressed couples do not differ in the number of conflicts they have, or even in what they fight about. Instead, they differ in how they argue and in how they think about conflict. Chapter 18 of your text discusses the effects on behavior of *attributions*, the explanations people make of their own and others' behavior. Attributions are critical in how people approach conflict, and affect whether they are satisfied or not in their relationships (Bradbury & Fincham, 1990; Holtzworth-Munroe & Jacobson, 1985). When contented people are irritated by their mates, they find reasons in the mate's temporary situation ("He's under a lot of pressure"). Distressed spouses, though, find reasons in the mate's personality ("He's thoughtless"). When people explain their mates' good behavior, though, their attributions reverse! Now happy couples look for reasons within the person ("She's so thoughtful to make my favorite meal"), and unhappy couples give credit to the situation ("She only makes a decent dinner when her mother pressures her to"). If you are thinking critically, you might wonder whether blaming your partner really leads to distress, or whether distress leads to blaming. Several studies, however, suggest that attributions do come first, and then affect satisfaction in the relationship (Bradbury & Fincham, 1990; Pines, 1986).

Happy and unhappy couples also differ in how they resolve their conflicts. Happy couples settle their disputes through discussion, compromise, and problem solving, the basic techniques of negotiation. They neither yield

31

every point nor bully the other side into submission. They are able to identify their goals, identify common interests, separate issues from personalities, and make short-term compromises for the sake of long-term gains (Pruitt & Rubin, 1986). Unhappy couples end up in repeated cycles of bickering and insults, blaming each other's faulty personality traits ("He's lazy"; "She's a nag").

You should not have too much difficulty recognizing the implications of findings on power, attributions, and negotiation in everyday life. Chances are you may have found yourself in this sort of situation: You watch your relationship with someone begin to deteriorate and it seems that everything you do only makes things worse. The findings we have been discussing suggest the following strategies to help pull your relationship out of its downward spiral:

- *Evaluate the explanations (attributions) you make of your partner's behavior.* Are you quick to blame him or her for some personality defect, while rarely crediting your partner with a personality strength? Do you consider how the situation might be influencing your partner's (and your own) behavior?

- *Analyze the relationship to find out whether inequity or an imbalance of power exists.* If you are feeling underloved, unappreciated, and underbenefited, you are likely to be feeling vaguely depressed or irritable. Does one of you make most of the decisions affecting you both? Does one of you have a financial advantage? Is one of you more invested emotionally in the relationship?

- *Examine whether you and your partner have different strategies f o r "getting your way."* A clash of methods may make communication difficult. If one of you is direct and assertive inexpressing your preferences, while the other withdraws and sulks,the two of you may end up quarreling over how to quarrel ("Lee's a bully"; "Chris is a sniveler"). Consider, too, whether your differences might be due to a lopsided distribution of power. One clue could be whether you get your way differently with different people. Are you forthright with your sister but cowardly with your sweetheart? Do you wheedle your way around your father but yell at your mother? If so, chances are that you feel less powerful with your sweetheart than your sister, and less with your father than your mother.

- *Negotiate your differences instead of resorting to bullying or blind submission.* As negotiation researcher Jeffrey Rubin once told us, "Negotiation requires patience and good will, but it is a pathway o f hope, an alternative to brutality, coercion, and submission. And i an also be a great deal of fun."

Assumption: *Women suffer more than men do at the end of a relationship.*

Thinking critically: Breakups are rarely easy for anyone, even when a person wants the breakup and even when both parties agree that the relationship wasn't very good (Berscheid, 1985; Brehm, 1992). One reason lies in the nature of human attachment. Attachment grows out of familiarity; it confers a feeling of connectedness with another. Although we usually associate attachment with committed, affectionate relationships, it also occurs in punishing, abusive ones. Mistreated children, spouses, and even pets may be strongly attached to those who abuse them. Couples may be emotionally attached to each other even when the emotions in question are negative ones, such as anger or anxiety. Such individuals are often surprised to find, on separation, more emotional attachment than they had anticipated (Berscheid, 1985).

Even so, studies suggest that men, contrary to stereotype, suffer at least as much, on the average, as women do, if not more (Riessman, 1990). In

33

the Boston Couples study, men reported *longer*-lasting grief after separation than the women did, even when the women had been more emotionally involved (Hill, Rubin, & Peplau, 1976). In another study, men and women were equally likely to become severely depressed after the divorce, but men were more likely to become depressed for the first time (Bruce & Kim, 1992).

A number of studies find that for women, the worst time emotionally is *before* the separation, whereas for men it is *after* the separation (Brehm, 1992). If you were a psychologist, what sorts of explanations might you consider testing to explain this finding?

One possibility is that women initiate breakups more than men do, and thus feel in more control of the situation. There is some evidence to support this idea (Goode, 1956; Hill et al., 1976; Spanier & Thompson, 1984). In one Canadian study of divorced couples, former spouses tended to agree that the woman had more control over the separation -- and perceiving oneself as having been in control was associated with better adjustment and lack of regret (Gray & Silver, 1990).

A second explanation is that women have more friends to help them deal with their distress after the break-up. Over the past two decades, many studies have found that married men tend to disclose their innermost feelings only to their wives. When these men divorce or separate, they may have no one to share their grief with.

A third explanation has to do with expectations (Brehm, 1992). Women are likely to be more aware of their financial dependency on a relationship, and may be more aware of their emotional dependency as well, so they may be better prepared for the losses they will face if the relationship ends. Men, however, often do not invest much time or energy in thinking about their relationships until it has fallen apart (Holtzworth-Munroe & Jacobson, 1985). As a result, they may not be aware of how dependent they have become on a partner for emotional and domestic

34

support -- and be traumatized when, after the separation, they are far more upset than they expected to be.

If you are thinking critically, you will realize that "suffering" can have different meanings, not all of them captured by a questionnaire on adjustment to a breakup. Men and women often have different problems after a divorce or separation-- differences not based on gender per se, but on power, income, and circumstances. For example, as we mentioned, after a breakup men often do not have a network of friends with whom they can share their pain and grief. They are also more likely, if they are fathers, to suffer the loneliness of the "Disneyland father" who only "visits" his children (Wallerstein & Blakeslee, 1989). On the other hand, most wives have more to lose economically after divorce than most husbands do. After "no-fault" divorce, women's disposable income falls 72 percent on the average while men's income rises 42 percent (Weitzman, 1985). How can this be? One reason is that women earn less than men in general. Another is that after divorce, most wives retain custody of the children and continue to have child-rearing expenses. Their former husbands, "freed" of family expenses, have more income to spend on themselves. Think critically about what you read or hear in the news. In spite of some sensational alimony awards, only 15 percent of all divorced women are awarded alimony (and only half of those actually get it), and the great majority of divorced fathers pay no child support. The result is that divorced women with children are among the poorest people in America. Can you think of any constructive ways to solve this growing problem?

As you can see, critical thinking requires that we reject glib generalizations, such as the common notion that one sex is "dependent" and the other "independent." Apparent independence may mask unrecognized dependence. Just as we are unaware of our dependency on oxygen until we can't get any air, we may be unaware of how dependent we are on a relationship -- and for what reason -- until we lose it.

Assumption: *Legal reforms and the fact that divorce is now so widespread have made divorce less stressful than it used to be.*

Thinking critically: Legal reforms do not necessarily affect the distress of separation, and the fact that separations are common does not necessarily make them easier to endure (Wallerstein & Blakeslee, 1989). People do not react casually to the breakups of major attachments, even when they choose the breakup or no longer feel close to the other person.

We once heard an exchange between a radio psychologist and a man who called in with this problem: He loved his wife, but he also was "in love" with another woman. How could he love two women, he wanted to know, and what should he do about it? In about 45 seconds, the radio psychologist got him to admit a preference for his woman friend. "No problem, then," she said. "Now that you know what you want, all you have to do is leave your wife."

The radio psychologist did not offer this man any information to help him think critically about his feelings and make an informed, if difficult, choice. She did not discuss research on romantic love, emotional attachments, the difficulty of separation, or the effects of divorce on children (as described in Chapter 13 of your text) or on the participants (as described in Chapter 14). She did not assess the man's own values about commitment or trust, though clearly he felt both toward his wife. For someone giving pop-psych advice, the answer was easy: If you want to leave a relationship, do it, and never mind the consequences.

It is not for us -- or the radio psychologist -- to say whether the man should or shouldn't have left his marriage. Ultimately, a decision of this sort must be based on your values and aspirations, and no amount of research can tell you what to do. But psychology, and critical thinking, can confer new perspectives on old problems. For example, it may be that our culture's emphasis on romantic passion has tended to obscure the need

36

for commitment and to underemphasize the strength of emotional attachments.

Relationships crumble for all sorts of reasons, including incompatible interests, boredom, poor communication, extramarital sex (or love), abuse and violence, or the emotional problems of one or both partners. Outside factors also affect the personal decision to part. Social as well as legal barriers to divorce have fallen in the last 20 years; more women are working and do not depend on their husbands for support, and religious opposition to divorce has diminished. Divorce has enabled many people to escape from painful, abusive, or deadening relationships. Yet divorce also produces much pain and unhappiness for all members of the family, at least in the short run and sometimes in the long run.

Over a decade ago, Ellen Berscheid and Bruce Campbell (1981) observed that easy divorce affects marriage in ways that are subtle but profound. As the cost of parting declines, people feel entitled to get more if they stay. As more and more marriages dissolve, the number of available partners increases, adding further pressure on a relationship to justify itself. "The freedom to stay or go has a price," said Berscheid and Campbell. "To have a perpetual choice means that one must choose--not once, but over and over again. And to do so, one must continually expend time and energy in evaluating and re-evaluating the wisdom of the choice."

Of course, if you have a choice, so does your partner. Knowing this may prevent a couple from talking their relationship for granted and behaving in thoughtless ways. But, observed Berscheid and Campbell, it also requires them to continually take the temperature of the relationship and worry about its health. And ironically, paying too much attention to the health of the relationship may help kill it.

37

THE FUTURE OF CLOSE RELATIONSHIPS

People often regard their close relationships as a safe haven in a stormy world. But the winds of change rock even the sturdiest boats. Attitudes about close relationships, and the roles we play in them, can change with dizzying speed.

In this handbook, we have encouraged you to challenge some assumptions about close relationships, and to look beyond obvious and oversimplified explanations of why close relationships do or do not succeed. We have pointed out how factors external to personality, from proximity to power, can affect relationships. You can use this information, along with your own ability to reason and draw conclusions, to speculate about the relationships of tomorrow. To get you started, we offer these possibilities:

- Similar interests draw people together and increase satisfaction in relationships. As gender roles have become more alike, men's and women's interests have converged -- on the job, in sports, in hobbies, in rearing children. If this trend continues, it should foster increased closeness between the sexes. But, as we might have predicted during economic hard times, we are also beginning to see, in some quarters, a renewed emphasis on traditional gender roles, which suggests that we could see some return to separate spheres of influence and interest.

- Power in relationships depends on each partner's resources. If women continue to become financially independent, male-female relationships may approach the balance of power that most people say they want. Yet women's financial independence depends on the availability of jobs (and of husbands) and on the nation's need for female labor. Economic changes could produce a return to traditional divisions of labor and therefore of power in the family.

- Physical attractiveness has a strong impact on people's impressions of strangers and choices of friends. In the United States, where people make frequent changes in jobs, cities, friends, and families, and where "the new" is more valued than tradition and "the old," individuals are often assessed quickly on the basis of how they look rather than on their record of behavior or their personal qualities. Perhaps this emphasis on youth and beauty will create difficulties for the long-term survival of relationships, since, as we saw, long-term relationships depend on trust, commitment, and realistic expectations. But perhaps, as the baby-boom generation ages, youth may become less valued and standards of beauty may change.

One thing is certain. In whatever form it occurs, intimacy with others will continue to offer both giant headaches and giant satisfactions. We hope that the use of critical thinking will help you minimize the headaches and increase the satisfactions in your own close relationships.

****

Now, here's a chance for you to practice your critical thinking skills by applying them to some real-world situations that people in close relationships often face. In each situation, see if you can identify some guidelines to critical thinking that might be applied to improve the probability of a happy outcome. (You may find it useful to refer back to the table on page 3.)

Situation #1

Herbie and Hermione have been going together for six months. They are no longer in the heart-pounding, knee-trembling phase of their romance, and Herbie concludes that his lack of fevered passion means he no longer loves Hermione. What principles of critical thinking can he use as he reevaluates their relationship?

Situation #2

Jezebel gets furiously jealous every time she sees her fiance, Jerome, talking to another woman -- which he seems to be doing a lot, lately. How should Jezebel go about analyzing this problem?

Situation #3

Lee and Pat have lived together for 15 years, and have always gotten along pretty well. But now they seem to be going through a slump in their relationship, and Lee is thinking of leaving. What should Lee consider before doing so?

Some suggested answers (but by no means the only ones):

1. Herbie can start by defining the problem. Has love really passed, or has he simply defined love too narrowly? Herbie may be making an unrealistic assumption about love: that heart-thumping passion can be permanent. But there are many ways to define love: as affection, intimacy, commitment, mutual support, trust. Herbie might also consider some alternative explanations for his ambivalence. Is he really "falling out of love," or is he uncomfortable about committing himself to any long-term relationship? Did he get involved with Hermione solely because of a physical attraction, without considering important differences in values and goals?

2. Jezebel needs, first and foremost, to resist emotional reasoning ("I'm consumed by feelings of jealousy, therefore I must have good reason to be jealous"). She also needs to examine the evidence for her assumption that Jerome is romantically interested in other women, and consider alternative interpretations. Perhaps Jerome really is straying, or wants to hurt Jezebel by flirting with other women. But he could simply be a sociable sort who likes talking to lots of people. Jezebel might also examine her own assumption that when a man talks to a woman his interest must be romantic or sexual. And she might analyze how her own reactions could be producing a self-fulfilling prophecy, by putting a strain on the relationship. In the end, Jezebel needs to decide whether her lack of trust is due to Jerome's behavior or her own needs and insecurities.

3. Lee might be making some unfounded assumptions: for example, that love and satisfaction in a relationship should always be constant (when in fact all relationships have their ups and downs), or that the grass is bound to be greener on the other side of the fence. Lee might also consider other possible explanations for the current situation, keeping in mind the human tendency to magnify dispositional attributions and ignore the effect of the situation. Perhaps Lee and Pat are feeling stressed not because of the relationship itself but because of problems with their children, their jobs, or their finances. Perhaps, having decided that they are bored with each other, they have stopped trying to introduce some excitement and enthusiasm into the relationship, and have therefore brought about a self-fulfilling prophecy.

41

REFERENCES

Acitelli, Linda K.; Douvan, Elizabeth; & Veroff, Joseph (1990).The importance of similarity and understanding to black and white newlyweds. Paper presented at the annual meeting of the American Psychological Association, Boston.

Antill, John K. (1983). Sex role complementarity versus similarity in married couples. *Journal of Personality and Social Psychology, 45*, 145-155.

Beer, William R (1984). *Househusbands: Men and housework in American families.* South Hadley, Mass.: J. F. Bergin.

Bernard, Jessie (1981). The good-provider role: Its rise and fall. *American Psychologist, 36*, 1-12.

Berscheid, Ellen (1985). Interpersonal attraction. In G. Lindzey & E. Aronson (eds.), *Handbook of social psychology, Vol II.* New York: Random House/Erlbaum.

Berscheid, Ellen, & Campbell, Bruce (1981). The changing longevity of heterosexual close relationships: A commentary and forecast. In M. Lerner (ed.), *The justice motive in times of scarcity and change.* New York: Plenum.

Berscheid, Ellen, & Walster, Elaine (1978). *Interpersonal attraction* (2nd edition). Reading, Mass.: Addison-Wesley.

Blood, Robert O., Jr., & Wolfe, Donald M. (1960). *Husbands and wives: The dynamics of married living.* New York: Free Press.

Blumstein, Philip, & Schwartz, Pepper (1983). *American couples.* New York: Morrow.

Botwin, Carol (1985). *Is there sex after marriage?* Boston, Mass.: Little, Brown.

Bradbury, Thomas N., & Fincham, Frank D. (1990). Attributions in marriage: Review and critique. *Psychological Bulletin*, 107, 3-33.

Brehm, Sharon S. (1992). *Intimate Relationships* (2nd ed.). New York: McGraw-Hill.

Bruce, Martha L., & Kim, Kathleen M. (1992). Differences in the effects of divorce on major depression in men and women. *American Journal of Psychiatry, 149*, 914-917.

Burda, Philip C, Jr.; Vaux, Alan; & Schill, Thomas (1984). Social support resources: Variation across sex and sex-role. *Personality and Social Psychology Bulletin*, 10, 119-126.

Burgess, Ernest W., & Wallin, Paul W. (1943). Homogamy in social characteristics. *American Journal of Sociology, 48*, 109 124.

Byrne, Donn (1971). *The attraction paradigm.* New York: Academic Press.

Camarena, Phame, & Sarigiani, Pamela (1985). Gender influences on intimacy development in early adolescence. Paper presented at the annual meeting of the American Psychological Association, Los Angeles, California

Campbell, Susan Rockwell, and Brown, Robert A. (1990). The relationship of interpersonal complementarity to marital satisfaction and security. Paper presented at the annual meeting of the American Psychological Association, Boston.

Cancian, Francesca M. (1987). *Love in America: Gender and self-development*. Cambridge, England: Cambridge University Press.

Carli, Linda L. (1990). Gender, language, and influence. *Journal of Personality and Social Psychology, 59*, 941-951.

Clark, Margaret S., & Reis, Harry T. (1988). Interpersonal processes in close relationships. *Annual Review of Psychology, 39*, 609-672.

Crosby, Faye (1986). Work. In C. Tavris (ed.), *EveryWoman's emotional well-being*. New York: Doubleday.

Dermer, Marshall & Thiel, Darrel (1975). When beauty may fail. *Journal of Personality and Social Psychology*, 31, 1168-1176.

Ebbesen, Ebbe B.; Kjos, Glen L.; & Konecni, Vladimir J. (1976). Spatial ecology: Its effects on the choice of friends and enemies. *Journal of Experimental Social Psychology, 12*, 505-518.

Falbo, Toni, & Peplau, Letitia A. (1980). Power strategies in intimate relationships. *Journal of Personality and Social Psychology, 38*, 618-628.

Feingold, Alan (1988). Matching for attractiveness in romantic partners and same-sex friends: A metaanalysis and theoretical critique. *Psychological Bulletin*, 104, 226-235.

Feingold, Alan (1992). Good-looking people are not what we think. *Psychological Bulletin, 111*, 304-341.

Feingold, Alan (1990). Gender differences in effects of physical attractiveness on romantic attraction: A comparison across five research paradigms. *Journal of Personality and Social Psychology*, 59, 981-993.

Festinger, Leon; Schachter, Stanley, & Back, Kun (1950). *Social pressures in informal groups: A study of human factors in housing*. New York: Harper & Brothers.

Goode, W.J. (1956). *After divorce*. Glencoe, IL: Free Press.

Gray, Janice D., & Silver, Roxane Cohen (1990). Opposite sides of the same coin: Former spouses' divergent perspectives in coping with their divorce. *Journal of Personality and Social Psychology, 59*, 1180-1191.

Gray-Little, Bernadette, & Burks, Nancy (1983). Power and satisfaction in marriage: A review and critique. *Psychological Bulletin, 93*, 513-538.

43

Hacker, Helen M. (1981). Blabbermouths and clams: Sex differences in self-disclosure in same-sex and cross-sex friendship dyads. *Psychology of Women Quarterly, 5*, 385-401.

Hatfield, Elaine (1984). The dangers of intimacy. In V. J. Derlega (ed.), *Communication, intimacy, and close relationships*. Orlando, Fla.: Academic Press.

Hatfield, Elaine; Traupmann, Jane; Sprecher, Susan; Utne, Mary; & Hay, Julia (1985). Equity and intimate relations: Recent research. In W. Ickes (ed.), *Compatible and incompatible relationships*. New York: Springer-Verlag.

Hill, Charles T.; Rubin, Zick; & Peplau, Letitia A. (1976). Breakups before marriage: The end of 103 affairs. *Journal of Social Issues, 32*, 147-168.

Hochschild, Arlie R. (1989). *The second shift: working parents and the revolution at home*. New York: viking.

Holtzworth-Munroe, Amy, & Jacobson, Neil S. (1985). Causal attributions of married couples: When do they search for causes? What do they conclude when they to? *Journal of Personality and Social Psychology, 48*,1398-1412.

Homans, George C (1961). *Social behavior: Its elementary forms*. New York: Harcourt.

Huston, Ted L (1983). Power. In H. H. Kelley, E. Berscheid et al. (eds.), *Close relationships*. New York: Freeman.

Johnson, Dennis J., & Rusbult, Caryl E. (1989). Resisting temptation: Devaluation of alternative partners as a means of maintaining commitment in close relationships. *Journal of Personality and Social Psychology, 57*, 967-980.

Jones, Warren H. (1982). Loneliness and social behavior. In L. A. Peplau & D. Perlman (eds.), *Loneliness: A sourcebook of current theory, research, and therapy*. New York: WileyInterscience.

Kalick, S. Michael, & Hamilton, Thomas E. (1986). The matching hypothesis reexamined. *Journal of Personality and Social Psychology, 51*, 673-682.

Kelley, Harold H.; Berscheid, Ellen; Christensen, Andrew; Harvey, John H.; Huston, Ted L.; Levinger, George; McClintock, Evie; Peplau, Letitia Anne; & Peterson, Donald R. (1983). *Close Relationships*. New York: Freeman.

Kipnis, David, & Schmidt, Stuart (1985). The language of persuasion. *Psychology Today*, 19(4), April, 40-46.

Klagsbrun, Francine (1985). Married people: Staying together In the age of divorce. Toronto and New York: Bantam.

Lakoff, Robin T. (1990). *Talking power: The politics of language*. New York: Basic Books.

Lauer, Jeanette, & Lauer, Robert (1986). *Til death do us part: How couples stay together*. New York: Haworth Press.

McElfresh, Stephen B. (1982). Conjugal power and legitimating norms: A new perspective on resource theory. Paper presented at the annual meeting of the American Psychological Association, Washington, D.C.

Miller, Rowland S., & Simpson, Jeffry A. (1990). Relationship satisfaction and attentiveness to alternatives. Paper presented at the annual meeting of the American Psychological Association, Boston.

Monge, Peter, & Kirste, Kenneth (1980). Measuring proximity in human organization. *Social Psychology Quarterly, 43*, 110-115.

Murstein, Bernard L (1982). Marital choice. In B. B. Wolman (ed.), *Handbook of developmental psychology*. Englewood Cliffs, N.J.: Prentice-Hall

Newcomb, Theodore (1961). *The acquaintance process*. New York: Holt, Rinehart, & Winston.
Nolen-Hoeksema, Susan (1991). Responses to depression and their effects on the duration of depressive episodes. Journal of Abnormal Psychology, 100, 569-582.

Peplau, Letitia A. (1984). Power in dating relationships. In J. Freedman (ed.), *Women: A feminist perspective* (3rd edition). Palo Alto, Cal: Mayfield.

Pines, Ayala M. (1986). Marriage. In C. Tavris (ed.), *EveryWoman's emotional well-being*. New York: Doubleday.

Pruitt, Dean, & Rubin, Jeffrey Z (1986). *Social conflict: Escalation, stalemate, and settlement*. New York: Random House.

Reis, Harry T.; Senchak, Marilyn; & Solomon, Beth (1985). Sex differences in the intimacy of social interaction: Further examination of potential explanations. *Journal of Personality and Social Psychology*, 48, 1204- 1217.

Reis, Harry T., & Shaver, Phillip (1988). Intimacy as an interpersonal process. In S. Duck (ed.), *Handbook of personal relationships: Theory, relationships and interventions*. New York: Wiley.

Rempel, John K.; Holmes, John G.; & Zanna, Mark P. (1985). Trust in close relationships. *Journal of Personality and Social Psychology, 49*, 95-112.

Riessman, Catherine (1990). *Divorce talk: Women and men make sense of personal relationships*. New Brunswick, NJ: Rutgers University Press.

Rubin, Zick; Peplau, Letitia A.; & Hill Charles (1981). Loving and leaving: Sex differences in romantic attachments. *Sex Roles, 7*, 821-835.

Schafer, Robert B., & Keith, Patricia M. (1980). Equity and depression among married couples. *Social Psychology Quarterly, 43*, 430-435.

Simpson, Jeffry A.; Gangestad, Steven W.; and Lerma, Margaret (1990). Perception of physical attractiveness: Mechanisms involved in the maintenance of romantic relationships. *Journal of Personality and Social Psychology, 59*, 1192-1201.

Snyder, Mark (1987). *Public appearances and private realities: The psychology of self-monitoring*. New York: W. H. Freeman.

Snyder, Mark; Berscheid, Ellen; & Glick, Peter (1985). Focusing on the exterior and the interior: Two investigations of the initiation of personal relationships. *Journal of Personality and Social Psychology, 48*, 1427-1439.

Solomon, Robert (1988). *About love*. New York: Simon & Schuster.

Spanier, Graham B., & Thompson, Linda (1984). *Parting: The aftermath of separation and divorce*. Beverly Hills, CA: Sage.

Sprecher, Susan (1986). The relation between inequity and emotions in close relationships. *Social Psychology Quarterly, 49*, 309-321.

Sprecher, Susan (1989). The importance to males and females of physical attractiveness, earning potential, and expressiveness in initial attraction. Sex Roles, 21, 591-607.

Sternberg, Robert J. (1985). A triangular theory of love. Paper presented at the annual meeting of American Psychological Association, Los Angeles, California.

Sternberg, Robert J. (1988). *The triangle of love: Intimacy, passion, commitment*. New York: Basic Books.

Tannen, Deborah (1990). *You just don't understand*. New York: William Morrow.

Tavris, Carol (1992). *The mismeasure of woman*. New York: Simon & Schuster.

Thibaut, John W., & Kelley, Harold H. (1959). *The social psychology of groups*. New York: Wiley.

Traupmann, Jane, & Hatfield, Elaine (1983). How important is marital fairness over the lifespan? *International Journal of Aging and Human Development, 17*, 89-101.

Traupmann, Jane; Petersen, R; Utne, Mary; & Hatfield, Elaine (1981). Measuring equity in intimate relations. *Applied Psychological Measurement, 5*, 467-480.

Waller, Willard (1938). *The family: A dynamic interpretation*. New York: Dryden.

Wallerstein, Judith, & Blakeslee, Sandra (1989). *Second chances: Men, women & children a decade after divorce*. New York: Ticknor & Fields.

Walster, Elaine; Aronson, Vera; Abrahams, Darcy; & Rottmann, Leon (1966). Importance of physical attractiveness in dating behavior. *Journal of Personality and Social Psychology, 4*, 508-516.

Walster, Elaine; Walster, George W.; & Berscheid, Ellen (1978). *Equity: Theory and Research*. Boston, Mass.: Allyn & Bacon.

Waring, Marilyn (1989). *If women counted: A new feminist economics*. San Francisco: Harper & Row.

Weitzman, Lenore (1985). *The divorce revolution: The unexpected social and economic consequences for women and children in America*. New York: The Free Press.

Wheeler, Ladd; Reis, Harry T.; & Nezlek, John (1983). Loneliness, social interaction, and sex roles. *Journal of Personality and Social Psychology, 45*, 843-853.

Wills, Thomas A.; Weiss, Robert L.; & Patterson, Gerald R. (1974). A behavioral analysis of the determinants of marital satisfaction. *Journal of Consulting and Clinical Psychology, 42*, 802-811.

Winch, Robert (1958). *Mate-selection: A study of complementary needs*. New York Harper.

Yllo, Kersti (1983). Sexual equality and violence against wives in American states. *Journal of Comparative Family Studies, 14*, 67-86.

Zajonc, Robert B. (1968). Attitudinal effects of mere exposure. *Journal of Personality and Social Psychology, 9, Monograph Supplement* (2, Part 2), 1-27.